CRITICAL GUIDES TO SPANISH TEXTS

5

Calderón de la Barca: El alcalde de Zalamea

CRITICAL GUIDES TO SPANISH TEXTS

Edited by

J. E. Varey and A. D. Deyermond

CALDERÓN DE LA BARCA

EL ALCALDE DE ZALAMEA

*

P. HALKHOREE

Lecturer in Spanish at Westfield College
University of London

Grant & Cutler Ltd

in association with

Tamesis Books Ltd

1972

Depósito legal: M.- 11.311-1972

Printed in Spain by Talleres Gráficos de Ediciones Castilla, S.A.
Maestro Alonso, 23 - Madrid

for

GRANT AND CUTLER LTD,
11, BUCKINGHAM STREET, LONDON, W.C.2.

Contents

Preface

El alcalde de Zalamea is one of Calderón's best-known and most immediately appealing works. Over the centuries, it has attracted the attention of students of the Spanish Golden Age theatre for various reasons. More recently, it has again been the subject of a number of studies, proving its ability to surprise critics by revealing ever-new facets. Moreover, since it is at first glance rather exceptional in the corpus of Calderón's plays and yet on closer examination reveals itself as typically Calderonian, it is an excellent introduction to this author's drama.

The play is well-nigh inexhaustible and the present book is intended to be no more than an introduction to the study of *El alcalde de Zalamea*. It attempts to take into account most, if not all, of the important work done on the play, with special emphasis on the most recent studies. It is hoped that what emerges is a reasonably coherent picture, which nevertheless avoids doing much injustice to the views of those critics on which it is largely based.

I have deliberately refrained from quoting from the text, preferring to give act-and-line references, not only in order to save space, but also in the expectation that the student will be reading this guide with the text of the play at hand in order to test the validity of my statements.

References to the text of the play are by Act (in Roman numerals) and lines (in Arabic numerals): for example, I.873-76 refers to Act I, lines 873-76. I have used the recent edition of the play by P. N. Dunn (Oxford: Pergamon Press, 1966), which is undoubtedly the most satisfactory English edition, and by now the standard one. The edition by J. Geddes (Boston: Heath and Co., 1918) coincides with

Dunn's in the numbering of the lines of each act. Students, therefore, who possess Geddes' edition should have no difficulty in locating the references. Bold numerals refer the reader to the Bibliography at the end of this study.

I wish to thank a number of persons who in various ways have helped to make the writing of this book possible: Professors J.E. Varey and A.D. Deyermond, the editors of this series, who read the original typescript and made several valuable suggestions for its improvement; Professor A. A. Parker, who clarified for me a point in his article, "Towards a Definition of Calderonian Tragedy", and who was also kind enough to discuss a number of aspects of the play with me; and, finally, my wife, Nelly, who has patiently read and criticised as many versions of this study as I was ready to produce: if it escapes being what she scathingly terms "a sterile academic exercise", it is due to her efforts.

None of the above, however, is to be held responsible for any of my views put forward here. In a number of instances, especially, I am conscious of having pushed my argument further than some of them would find acceptable. For such aberrations and eccentricities I bear full responsibility.

P.H.
London, 1971.

I

Introduction

Calderón's plays mark the culmination of the development of the Spanish Golden Age *comedia,* the form of which was established in the late sixteenth century by Lope de Vega. A formal description of the *comedia* is not difficult: it is in three acts, in verse, and employs a variety of metres. It is also a non-classical type of drama, that is, it does not observe the basic neo-classical rules concerning the three unities of time, place and action, the rigid separation of tragic from comic elements, the separation of styles, and the separation of characters according to social class. Such is the dramatic form Calderón inherited and used unchanged.

If the form of the *comedia* remained unchanged, the same cannot be said of its structure, style and content. In these areas, the overall movement (clearly discernible in the production of Lope de Vega) was towards technical perfection, more pronounced artificiality, and greater intellectualism. All these features are present in Calderón's plays almost from the start.

The internal structure of the *comedia* underwent considerable development, largely as a result of criticism by the neo-classical theorists, who saw the early *comedias* as artistically unsatisfactory works. Calderón's plays, however, could hardly merit this criticism: even his early ones reveal a technical perfection which could at times be equalled, but was never surpassed, by the works of his contemporaries. His search for technical perfection (amply demonstrated by A. E. Sloman in his important work *The Dramatic Craftsmanship of Calderón*, Oxford, 1958) is clear even from a quick glance at his plays. These reveal a move towards a tighter, more economical, more unitary structure in which nothing could be regarded as superfluous. In fact, as Sloman has remarked (18, p.297), Calderón's plays, in a sense, become more classical. (*El alcalde de Zalamea*, as we shall see, is an interesting example of this tendency.) The looser, often episodic structure of Lope's earliest plays was replaced by the rigorously logical, causal structure of Calderón's plays. The arrangement of scenes and incidents in the latter is also very carefully worked out, with the maximum exploitation of parallels, contrasts, and devices that anticipate new developments or look back to earlier stages in the plot.

The natural consequence of such developments was a dramatic form which became increasingly artificial. The fresher, apparently "spontaneous" style of the early Lope gives way to a highly artificial style which owes much to Gongorism and to *culteranismo* (that is, the use of a learned or *culto* style) in general.[1] A systematic and organic use of imagery for thematic and structural purposes, parallelisms, contrasts, cumulative series of images, etc. are standard features of Calderón's style. Another instance of his calculated approach to play-writing is his re-working of earlier plays. In fact, *El alcalde de Zalamea* is itself such a re-working of an earlier play of the same name.

This artificiality in the style and structure of Calderón's plays is not to be seen as a mere display of technical virtuosity but rather as marking a movement away from a more "realistic" to a "symbolic" form of drama, that is, a dramatic form which, by virtue of its comparative indifference to surface realism, was an adequate vehicle for Calderón's thought. Calderón's drama is, in fact, profoundly intellectual.

In the field of thought, also, Calderón's plays mark the culmination of the Golden Age *comedia*. That the *comedia* should have been born in the late sixteenth century was significant, for thus it was inevitably influenced by the atmosphere of the Counter-Reformation

---

[1] For a good introductory discussion of Gongorism and *culteranismo* see pp. xxxvi ff. of the Introduction to Part II of A. Terry, *An Anthology of Spanish Poetry* (Oxford, 1968).

which called for more responsible, moral, and "realistic" art. Even if it can be argued that some of the early *comedias* were more realistic than responsible or moral, there is no doubt that the general trend, aided by the moralists' severe criticism of the Golden Age theatre (which continued throughout the seventeenth century), was towards a form of drama embodying moral and Christian principles, that is, a form of art in which the main emphasis was laid on the first of the two Horatian aims of art: to instruct and to delight. This trend clearly culminates in Calderón's works, most obviously in his *autos sacramentales*, but also in his secular plays.

Every artist is, to some extent, a mirror of his times, and Calderón is no exception. His dramatic world reflects the sense of crisis which was undoubtedly felt in Spain (and the rest of Europe) in the seventeenth century. The world in which Calderón's plays move is a complex and puzzling one: hence the frequent occurrence of words such as "confusion", "labyrinth", etc. It is a world in which man, by himself, can hardly cope, a world, therefore, in which faith is essential.

Within this body of highly stylised, basically non-realistic plays, *El alcalde de Zalamea* appears, at first sight, to be something of an anomaly. The penultimate line refers to "esta historia verdadera". This is, admittedly, puzzling. Sloman's view is as follows:

> The first *El alcalde de Zalamea* [Sloman is referring to the source-play on which Calderón's *El alcalde* is based] is concerned with a peasant whose daughters were seduced by two captains who pass through Zalamea on their way to Portugal in 1580. It was based probably upon an actual incident which occurred at that time in Zalamea, though Krenkel has shown its resemblance to the forty-seventh tale of the *Novellino* of Masuccio Guardati of Salerno (18, p.218).

P. N. Dunn, however, in the notes to his edition of the play, comments:

> this phrase is not true in any narrow sense. The play is not the dramatic reconstruction of a real historical incident. Philip II did not go to Zalamea, nor did Don Lope de Figueroa. It is a true history in the sense that it is a representation of what is possible

within the historical circumstances which it reflects.   The
depredations of the soldiery billeted on a civilian population
whom they despised were a normal hazard for which there was
usually no redress, for "military tribunals winked at the offences
of their men, and the highest tribunal of all, the Council of War,
could be relied upon to take the part of its captains and *maestres
de campo*" (J. H. Elliott, *Imperial Spain* (London, 1964), p.289)
(**1**, p. 140).

Whether the story is factually accurate or not is, however, probably
of little real importance for an understanding of the play.   But
Calderón's words do draw attention to his realistic handling of the
story.

The realism of *El alcalde de Zalamea* has never passed unnoticed by
critics (**10**, pp.226-27).   A mere glance at the opening scene suffices
to convince us of the validity of this view.   The play abounds in
action and colour; the characters strike us as "real" persons; the action
is clearly localised in and near a specific village, and involves people
who bear an obvious resemblance to persons one might have met in
a seventeenth-century Spanish village.   But while no one would wish
to discount this genuinely "realistic" aspect of *El alcalde de Zalamea*,
it must be admitted that the play is less of an exception than it at
first seems.   Like virtually all of Calderón's plays, *El alcalde de
Zalamea* is a highly artificial work, whose surface realism is the care-
fully-planned product of a master craftsman.   This artificiality of
El alcalde has only comparatively recently been stressed, and it might
be a good idea to examine the play to see how artificial its realism is.
The paradox might seem gratuitous at this stage, but, once we start
looking closely at the play, we realise that paradox is one of its most
basic and exciting features.

II

El alcalde de Zalamea: a refundición

Calderón's *El alcalde de Zalamea*, like a number of his more important plays, is a re-working, or *refundición*, of an earlier play bearing the same title. Early critics had tended to see in Calderón's *refundiciones* little more than plagiarisms, but A. E. Sloman established once and for all that these *refundiciones*, far from being mere plagiarisms, were one clear manifestation of Calderón's unceasing search for dramatic perfection (18).

Calderón did not simply touch up existing plays and pass them off as his own. His *refundiciones* constitute entirely new plays, irrespective of whether he took over the basic structure of his source-play or merely the general situation. In some cases, indeed, as with *La vida es sueño*, Calderón's play is so different from the source that his debt for long went unperceived. *El alcalde de Zalamea* is a play which illustrates perfectly how Calderón could transform a dramatically unsophisticated and thematically simple work into a highly complex and profound drama.

Two plays, both bearing the title of *El alcalde de Zalamea*, exist: Calderón's play and one attributed to Lope de Vega, although Morley and Bruerton consider it unlikely that the latter play is in fact by Lope.[2] Valbuena has suggested that this latter play is later than Calderón's, arguing that it is structurally and technically superior.[3] Sloman's analysis proves, however, that this argument is untenable: Calderón's play is undoubtedly superior. Moreover, as Sloman remarks, the versification of the play attributed to Lope points to a

2 S. G. Morley and C. Bruerton, *The Chronology of Lope de Vega's* Comedias (New York, 1940).
3 A. Valbuena Prat, *Historia del teatro español* (Barcelona, 1965), p.271.

date before 1610 (**18**, p.218). Knowing Calderón's tendency to re-
write existing plays which he considered unsatisfactory, though
potentially good, we can therefore conclude with some confidence
that Calderón's *El alcalde de Zalamea* is the later play.

A couple of other factors may help us to date Calderón's work.
As has often been pointed out (e.g., **1**,p.7), the news of Portugal's
independence would have been widely known in Spain by 1644 and
it is therefore unlikely that a play dealing with Philip II's journey to
Portugal to be crowned would have been staged after that date.

The second factor is this: it has been argued that the scenes of army
life in *El alcalde de Zalamea* are so vivid and authentic that they very
probably derived from first-hand experience. Excessive weight ought
not to be given to this theory, but Calderón did take part in the war
with Catalonia in the years 1640-42. If he drew upon this experience
in writing the relevant scenes of *El alcalde*, this would point to a date
of composition between 1642 and 1644. Moreover, we are dealing
with a very skilfully written play in which Calderón's complete and
unobtrusive mastery of his medium is amply demonstrated. This,
too, would argue against an early date.

There is one crucial fact, however, which must be taken into
account. J. E. Varey and N. D. Shergold have brought to light a
reference to a palace performance of a play called *El alcalde de
Zalamea* in 1636.[4] Unfortunately, there is nothing in the documentary
source to indicate whether this play is Calderón's or the one attributed
to Lope, the author not being mentioned. Varey and Shergold
conclude that this performance may well be of the Lope play,
although, of course, certainty here is impossible.

To sum up, then, most of the evidence seems to indicate that
Calderón's *El alcalde de Zalamea* was written in the early 1640's. The
play attributed to Lope appears to have been written around 1610.
It is reasonable to conclude, therefore, as Sloman has done, that

---

[4] N. D. Shergold and J. E. Varey, "Some Early Calderón Dates", *Bulletin of
Hispanic Studies,* 38 (1961), 275-76.

Calderón's work is a *refundición* of the play attributed to Lope.

As Sloman points out, the source play is essentially a work about an *alcalde* and about justice, whereas Calderón's play is primarily about honour (18, p.226). In order to achieve this shift in thematic emphasis, Calderón had to alter his source play considerably. In doing so, he also produced a more unified, tightly-knit and satisfactory drama. A comparison of Calderón's play with its source can help to illustrate his dramatic skill more clearly and also bring the theme of the play into clearer focus. This is what Sloman does in chapter 8 of his work (18). I summarize his findings below.

In the source play, the protagonist, Pedro Crespo, is elected *alcalde* at the outset, and most of the exposition is concerned with his acts of justice. His daughters, Inés and Leonor, flirt with the captains of the companies billeted in Zalamea, Don Juan and Don Diego. An attempt by the daughters to elope with the Captains is foiled by Crespo, who arrests a sergeant. In Act II, Crespo's punishment of the sergeant meets with the approval of Don Lope de Figueroa. Crespo, however, indicates that other officers are even more guilty, but declines to expatiate on this. The Captains take revenge by persuading Inés and Leonor to elope with them. Then they seduce and abandon the girls. In Act III, the daughters appeal to the *alcalde* for justice, producing the Captains' written promises of marriage. Crespo, on going to arrest some soldiers about whom a peasant has complained, discovers that they are the Captains. He compels them to marry the girls, in accordance with their written promises. When Philip II arrives, he is shown the Captains hanging from the gallows. Crespo explains that they have had to suffer this ignominious form of death because of the executioner's lack of experience in beheading. Crespo is made *alcalde* for life and his daughters enter a convent.

It will be evident that, while Calderón's play appears similar in general outline to the source *El alcalde*, the two plays, as a closer examination reveals, have little in common. Calderón's specific debt to his source is limited. Of the action of the play, only the last scene was retained. Of the characters, it is Lope alone who remains virtually intact in Calderón's play. Pedro Crespo, Isabel and the Captain (and, to some extent, the Sergeant) are borrowed only nominally from the source, for their characters have been quite transformed. All the other characters are new. It is clear, therefore, even at this superficial level of comparison, that Calderón has written a new and original play.

Furthermore, it is equally clear that Calderón has been original in the handling of his borrowed material. As regards the *denouement*, Calderón, while retaining the last scene of his source, changes virtually all the rest of the material. The last scene, therefore, needs to be viewed in a new context. In the source, it was an unsatisfactory *dénouement* to the play both morally and artistically. In Calderón, the final scene stresses the contrast between the moral law and the law of the state, a contrast which is fundamental to the whole play. Whereas, in the source, Pedro Crespo acted throughout in an official capacity, Calderón avoided writing a play about an *alcalde*'s acts of justice. He, however, preserved the *coup de théâtre* by postponing Crespo's election until Act III. We are thus presented with a different view of Crespo, and one which renders much of the source-material superfluous.

As Sloman remarks, Calderón's principal debt to his source is for the outlines of his main characters. Calderón's Pedro Crespo is a man of honour, more noble and dignified than the character in the source play, while new touches are added: he is shrewd and a good father to his two children. The two daughters of the source are reduced to one in Calderón's play, namely Isabel. Her character has been changed: she is a virtuous, prudent daughter, whose sense of honour links her to her father. Her cousin, Inés, slightly less reserved, takes the place of the second daughter. Juan is a new creation. According to Sloman, he, along with Crespo and Isabel, completes the picture of integrity and honour. He is in some respects like, in others unlike, his father.

Of the other characters, Álvaro's rôle is taken over from the source, but his character is different. Don Lope is unchanged. In many ways, he resembles the new Crespo. Calderón enlarged his rôle and "made him an essential part of the play's pattern". As A. A. Parker has remarked, Lope upholds the outward forms of honour; Crespo its inner essence (12). Rebolledo and La Chispa are new creations who fill out the picture of the soldiery. They, too, have their own conception of honour: honour for them is a matter exclusively of reputation and bravado. Mendo and Nuño are also new; they provide humour and continuity. But, in addition, Mendo's concept of honour is false and hollow, not having even the dubious social value of Rebolledo's. He stands in contrast to the Captain.

The originality of Calderón's play is further illustrated if one compares the basic situations in the source with those in his play. Most of Act I of Calderón's *El alcalde* is new. The clash of Crespo and Lope at the end owes something to the source, but in Calderón's play it occurs in different circumstances and brings out the full measure of Crespo's stature. Calderón's second act has very little in common with the source. In Act III, the general situation and some lines have a parallel in the source; but the details of the situation are very different. Crespo is appointed *alcalde* and has to clear his honour in a way compatible with his new position.

The effect of all these changes is, as Sloman concludes, to present us with characters who give the impression of being real people. The structure is also much improved: it possesses a coherence and unity lacking in the earlier play. There are frequent hints which foreshadow the *dénouement*. The principle of causality is clearly at work in the play, which emphasises the question of moral responsibility. The language of the play is new. The imagery owes little or nothing to the source and is typically Calderonian. The verse-forms are all different and the use of music and songs is also original. The staging of the final *coup de théâtre* is changed.

In short, Calderón's play is a "study of a peasant's honour". His debt to his source consists of the basic facts of the story, the *dénouement*, and the outlines of the four main characters. The rest is new and original: the whole of the structure is new, only a small proportion of the original material being kept in Calderón's *refundición*.

Themes

The themes of the play are, as Dunn has stated, honour, justice and love. "But", Dunn continues, "a play is made of more than just such generalities. The peculiar mode in which these ideas are presented is due to their becoming crucial issues in the life of an imagined man, Pedro Crespo, and matters of conflict between him and other characters" (1, p.10). It is through the characters and the relationships between them that these themes are presented, explored and worked out.

The central theme is, of course, honour. This is in accordance with Lope de Vega's recommendation that:

> Los casos de la honra son mejores,
> porque mueven con fuerza a toda gente.
>
> (*Arte nuevo de hacer comedias*, lines 328-29)

But it has been suggested that the theme of honour is not central to this play. Margaret Wilson, for example, argues that *El alcalde de Zalamea* should be distinguished from those plays which involve the murder of a wife by a suspicious husband (22, p.154). To argue thus, however, is probably to define the phenomenon of honour too narrowly. As has been made clear in a recent study, honour involves all the values of a society (15). Furthermore, *El alcalde de Zalamea* is not a daughter-murder play only because Pedro Crespo is a wiser, more prudent father than are the husbands in the wife-murder plays, and it is saved from becoming a sister-murder play only by Crespo's timely intervention in Act III.

Nevertheless, the question of honour is a vexed one. The wife-murder plays have led some critics to comment on the immorality of a culture which approved of such an act, of plays which seemingly commended the act to the public, and of authors who wrote plays in which such acts were presented in a favourable light (**10**, pp.229-33). However, more modern critics have suggested, more reasonably, that such a view is erroneous. Wife-murders, they argue, are not approved of. Calderón's purpose was to present a critique of the code of honour which led to such senseless acts.[5] C. A. Jones, however, has argued that the code of honour was simply a convenient dramatic device which allowed the dramatists to explore other problems.[6]

The last two views are not necessarily mutually exclusive. Calderón doubtless found the honour code a useful dramatic device which allowed him to explore problems; but one of these problems was, surely, the question of honour itself. While it is probably true to say that Calderón does not condemn outright the code of honour, he assuredly does make us aware of its limitations. *El alcalde de Zalamea* is no exception to this.

In this play, Calderón presents different facets of honour. The term "honour", of course, is ambiguous. Not only does it refer to one's innate nobility, but even more importantly in Calderón's day, it signified basically a man's reputation in society, a reputation which depended partly on his possessing and being seen to possess those values and qualities of which his society approved and partly on his own opinion of himself. Thus a definition of honour must involve social as well as moral and personal values. Calderón paints a series of characters in whom these elements are present in varying proportions, ranging from the high-born Mendo to the peasant Crespo. He explores the different types of honour through these characters,

[5] See, e.g., E. M. Wilson, "Gerald Brenan's Calderón", *Bulletin of the Comediantes*, 4, No. 1 (1952), 6-8.

[6] In the following articles: "*Honor* in Spanish Golden-Age Drama: Its Relation to Real Life and to Morals", *Bulletin of Hispanic Studies*, 35 (1958), 199-210; and "Spanish Honour as Historical Phenomenon, Convention and Artistic Motive", *Hispanic Review*, 33 (1965), 32-39.

searching for the most satisfactory definition of honour. He ultimately produces a situation in which a distinction has to be made between honour as social reputation and honour as moral integrity, a situation, moreover, in which the two definitions of honour are seen as mutually incompatible.

The themes of justice and love help to create this situation. Love too, is presented from different angles through the various characters. It is mostly presented in its unruly aspects —in Mendo and the Captain, for example: these, claiming to love Isabel, are in reality only interested in satisfying their own lust; they exemplify love in its varieties of self-love. But its better, more harmonious side is not wholly absent. There is Crespo's paternal affection and the filial love of Juan and Isabel; there is also the mutual respect and affection of Crespo and Lope. Perhaps the only aspects missing are those of husband for wife (seldom presented on the Golden Age stage in any case) and a true, noble relationship between lovers. It is the violent aspects of love which bring the play's definition of honour clearly into focus and also produce crises in the nobler forms of love. Justice, the third theme, is also brought into conflict with honour; in fact, Calderón engineers a situation in which justice and honour are shown to be incompatible. Justice also comes into conflict with love: Pedro Crespo, as *alcalde*, must imprison his son, Juan, and publicly expose Isabel's shame.

These three themes are brought into conflict and the implications explored by their being presented through the characters. This aspect of the play will be examined next.

Characters

As critics have pointed out, the Spanish *comedia* subordinates character-drawing to action, and action to theme.[7] Two consequences follow from this: first, the characters must be seen in functional terms, that is, in terms of what they contribute to the action and how their acts help to elucidate the theme; secondly, verisimilitude is a relatively unimportant consideration because of the principal importance of the theme.

However, in the matter of characterisation, as in so many other respects, *El alcalde de Zalamea* is something of an exception. This is not to imply that the characterisation is, in itself, the most important aspect of the play, but that the characters perhaps convey a more vivid sense of being real persons than is usual in many of Calderón's plays. This may be so, paradoxically, because they are drawn with simple, strong lines. Our impression of them is not that they are complex beings whose personalities are largely hidden from us, whose motives and thoughts we must puzzle out. On the contrary, they are strong, elemental beings, true to themselves, and thus possessed of a certain integrity of character. Even the Captain, misguided though his attitude is, remains true to himself to the end.

The gallery of characters in the play ranges from the King through nobles to the peasants. We are thus presented with a cross-section of society: this is not primarily in the interests of a greater realism (although it must contribute to that) but for two main reasons: first, the themes of the play are thereby universalised, since they are presented as affecting all classes of society, and, secondly, a more

[7] E g., E.M. Wilson, *"La vida es sueño", Revista de la Universidad de Buenos Aires,* 3a época, año IV, Nos 3 and 4 (1946), 61-78. Reprinted in Wardropper (19).

searching exploration of the themes themselves and especially of the central theme of honour is made possible.

Pedro Crespo, the protagonist of the play, is a peasant. In this he is something of an anomaly in the plays of Calderón, whose heroes are normally drawn from the upper classes. But, as Sloman points out, Crespo is dignified (18, pp. 228-29), a fact which is made obvious by a comparison with the *alcalde* of the source play. Calderón's hero is not presented to us primarily as an *alcalde* but as a morally noble, worthy and respected peasant. These are important traits in his portrayal as a man of honour. He gives us his famous definition of honour towards the end of Act I (I.874-76). But this does not mean that he is indifferent to social honour. From the words of Mendo and Nuño and the Sergeant, we learn that Crespo is the richest man in Zalamea (I.165-67; 317-28), has the best house in the village (I.174-75), and is proud (I.168-71). That he is a good swordsman is made clear by the fact that he can hold his own with Don Lope (II.457-58). He is a good and solicitous father, as is shown in his farewell speech to Juan (II.682-744), by his decision to conceal Isabel (I.523-40), and by his humane treatment of her after she has been raped.

It is because of these sound qualities, no doubt, that he is held in high esteem by his fellow-villagers. His election as *alcalde* is proof of this fact. That he is extremely conscious of his reputation comes out in his advice to Juan (I.452-58; II.686ff). He is a man of integrity and conscious of being so. Hence his refusal to buy a patent of nobility (I.485-521). He is proud of his status as a peasant and recognises his obligations as such. But he refuses to be persuaded into thinking that as a man he is innately inferior to those who belong to a superior social class. This is indicated clearly by his declarations to Lope (I.850ff). In the second act, he insists on his equality with other men (II.235-44).

At the same time, it is hard not to see Crespo as rather proud, even arrogant. And surely it is his opinion of himself as an honest, respectable man of integrity which is at the centre of his pride, in other words, his concern with his social reputation. This concern for social honour is, of course, slightly at odds with his theoretical definition of honour as moral integrity; but if the latter is what he regards, in his *fuero interno*, as true and valid, the play shows him what its full implications are.

Juan is to a large extent like Crespo; the real difference between them lies in the fact that Juan is, as is to be expected, more immature. He has all the impetuosity and rashness of youth and it is these which he must learn to curb. His concept of honour is basically the same as his father's (I.765-70). But he lays more stress on the conventional aspect of it. Thus he is prepared to kill Isabel, and only Crespo's timely appearance prevents him from doing so in Act III. He has still to learn what prudence is, but no doubt the events in the play teach him, as they do us, something about its nature. And we do see him learning in the way in which he puts into effect —though at times imperfectly— his father's advice.

Isabel, like her father and brother, is also very conscious of her honour. She rejects Mendo's pathetic attempts at courtship and is distressed by the soldiers' crude serenade in Act II. She shows prudence in thinking, as does Crespo, that she ought to remain in her room while soldiers are in the house, thus contrasting with the more lively Inés. Like Juan, she tends to have a more conventional sense of honour, fully expecting her father to kill her once she has told him of her rape (III.267-80), and she is as astounded as Juan when Crespo decides to make her shame public by asking her to file a complaint against the Captain.

If the above three characters represent a notion of honour held by the peasants, Don Lope stands for the honour of the soldiers. Like Pedro Crespo, he is a man of integrity who is willing to listen, at times, to another man's point of view (I.877-78). He is jealous of his authority and resents any attempt to encroach upon it. Like Crespo, he is obstinate and stands on his rights. But he tries to be just and fair to all: witness his order to the soldiers to leave Zalamea after the incident in front of Crespo's house. He also assures Crespo at the end of the play that he would have seen to it that the Captain was punished for the rape of Isabel.

Apart from this, Lope is also shown as a kindly and civil person. He realises that in Crespo he has met his match and someone very much like himself. Their initial aggressiveness soon turns into mutual respect in Act II. Lope, also, unlike the other soldiers, is courteous to Isabel, and is as offended as Crespo by the soldiers' serenade.

The Captain, the villain of the piece, is a man of strong passions. He is contemptuous of peasants to whom he denies all honour. This attitude persists to the last when he rejects Crespo's plea to him to marry Isabel. His social arrogance is based on his concept of honour. His contempt for the peasants might only have produced uncivil behaviour on his part, but his tragedy is that he experiences an over-whelming passion for Isabel. When he realises that she will have nothing to do with him, he resorts to violence and then abandons her.

While he thus complacently violates moral and civil laws where a person of a lower class is concerned, he makes a great point about the niceties of civil law where he himself is involved. To the last, he seems to trust to his theoretical immunity from civil law, stressing that he is outside its jurisdiction. But he has behaved in an unworthy manner and suffers a form of execution normally reserved for the members of the class he despises so much.

The Sergeant plays a comparatively minor part in the play: he is the Captain's accomplice. He shares the Captain's contempt for the lower classes, but has not Don Álvaro's fastidiousness (I.179-203). Lower-class women are obviously mere instruments of pleasure for him. But from the point of view of the mechanics of the plot, he is important in that it is he who billets the Captain on Pedro Crespo, knowing that the latter has a beautiful daughter with whom the Captain may want to amuse himself.

Rebolledo and La Chispa are two of the play's more colourful characters. Chispa has her own sense of honour. She is no helpless woman (I.65-85), and aspires to be "la bolichera" (I.629-30; 650-52). Rebolledo is a boastful soldier with a history of desertion of which he is proud (I.37-44). He, like Crespo, is conscious of the need to clear his debts in order to maintain his social honour (cf. I.453-58 and I.621-26). But honour for him is not something which can stand in the way of narrow self-interest: threatened with torture by Lope, he reveals that the story of a quarrel with the Captain was a complete fabrication (I.815-29).

Mendo, from the social point of view the most honourable character in the village, is, from the moral point of view, the man whose conception of honour is the most hollow. For him, honour lies in his possession of a patent of nobility (I.259-64). Like the Captain, he despises the peasants, but, like the Sergeant, he is not averse to considering using peasant-women (Isabel) for his own amusement. The seduction of Isabel which he plans in his fantasy and which he is too powerless to execute is carried out by the Captain in a more brutal fashion when his passion overwhelms him. Mendo is a pathetic character, whose hollow declarations and statements are systematically punctured by Nuño with his sharp and pitiless puns.

The last two characters, Inés and the King, need not detain us long. The King performs a purely formal rôle in the play, the significance of which will be examined later. He is (perhaps unusually for Calderón) presented in a favourable light as the administrator of justice. Inés acts as a foil to Isabel, thus serving to accentuate the latter's qualities. Inés is the more flighty of the two (though no less virtuous); she is a bit saucy —witness her remark in I.553-56. She reacts with presence of mind when Isabel is abducted by fetching Crespo's sword. And her more worldly-wise, matter-of-fact attitude to life attempts to provide Isabel with some consolation (III.650-54).

As will have become evident from the above considerations, we are meant to compare and contrast the characters in the play in order to follow Calderón's exploration of the nature of honour. As Dunn remarks: "In *El alcalde de Zalamea* Calderón presents a series of variations on the theme of *honra* which all contrast with [one another and with] the central, just view taken by Pedro Crespo" (1, p.13). In other words, we are presented with a series of tentative definitions of honour, working our way from Mendo to Pedro Crespo, each more meaningful than the last, until we get what promises to be the fullest definition of honour in Crespo. But, as Dunn points out, honour for Crespo does not ignore social reputation (1, p.15). Nevertheless, is this the fullest definition of honour? If so, what of honour as "patrimonio del alma"? We —and Pedro Crespo— have to discover the nature of this type of honour. It is brought out by the way the situation is developed in the plot.

V

The Plot and Its Meaning

The *comedia* as a whole is an art-form with certain basic artistic principles and with a fairly well-defined aim. Because of this, A. A. Parker has been able to formulate a set of principles which can aid us in our study of the Golden Age *comedia* in general, and especially of the plays of Calderón **(11)**. These are as follows:

1. The primacy of action over character drawing;
2. The primacy of theme over action;
3. Dramatic unity in the theme and not in the action;
4. The subordination of the theme to a moral purpose through the principle of poetic justice;
5. The elucidation of the moral purpose by means of dramatic causality.

In a later article, Parker draws attention to a specific type of Calderonian tragedy, based on the principle of "diffused responsibility" **(14)**. This is a type of tragedy in which there is no clear-cut villain, but in which the catastrophe is brought about by the concatenation of the results of the actions (which may in themselves be relatively innocent) of a number of persons.

While this latter article has generally been regarded as a most important contribution to the study of Calderonian tragedy, the five principles set forth in *The Approach* have recently been subjected to a certain amount of criticism. (For a critique of Parker's views, see **16** in the Bibliography.) Nevertheless, the application of Parker's five principles can often be of considerable help in studying a play. The following analysis of *El alcalde de Zalamea* is based to some extent on these principles. It will also be seen that there exists in the play a network of relationships which makes one think of Parker's "diffused responsibility". But, since there is a clear-cut villain in the play, Parker himself would not apply diffused responsibility here.

A Golden Age play, according to Parker, should exemplify poetic justice. As he explains:

> Poetic justice is a principle of literature and not a fact of experience. In real life evil men may prosper and virtuous men may suffer. But in literature it was, in seventeenth-century Spain, considered fitting that wrongdoing should not go unpunished and that virtue should not remain unrewarded. The Spanish drama also implicitly asserts the converse of the necessary punishment of the evildoer, namely that nobody should be punished, should suffer disaster, without deserving it (11, p.7).

Now, if we examine the ending of *El alcalde* in this light, we must be careful not to oversimplify. There is suffering enough by the end of the play: of that there is no doubt. The most obvious example is the Captain's death. But Pedro Crespo and his family, too, have to bear suffering. Isabel has been raped; this has had to be made public for the Captain's trial to be just and legal, and she has to enter a convent, her dishonour unavenged, her suffering unalleviated, her life in society ruined. Juan, too, is in gaol until the last moments of the play, and is released only at Lope's request. Crespo himself has had to acknowledge his dishonour publicly in order to ensure that justice is done. True, the King restores his social honour by making him *alcalde perpetuo*, but even so, this cannot undo the suffering he must undergo as a result of the events in the play. Even Lope suffers a certain amount of frustration by the indignity of having one of his captains executed like a common criminal. To decide whether poetic justice is exemplified in all this suffering, it will be necessary to attempt to trace the pattern of cause and effect in the plot.

If we try to work back from the end, using the principle of causality, in order to find out how such suffering is brought about, we discover an interesting pattern. The main causal strand, of course, links the Captain's execution with his moral guilt. His dishonourable death is certainly merited: he is guilty of having raped Isabel, of having rejected Crespo's offer, of being offensively arrogant, of having, in short, been the principal cause of virtually all the suffering in the play.   There is no doubt that he is the villain of the piece, and his death, then, exemplifies poetic justice.

But, probing further, we see that, while the Captain, by reason of his clear-cut moral guilt, must bear the main responsibility for his death, others have contributed towards producing the initial situation. Here the network of secondary causal relationships becomes more complex and invests the play with a deep tragic irony.   The Captain dies because he rejected Crespo's offer, having raped Isabel.   He abducted and raped her because she refused to consider his advances, being a respectable and virtuous daughter.   He tried to court her because of his overwhelming passion for her, which arose when he first saw her.   As he himself says, his love was all the more violent because he never expected to see such a beautiful peasant girl.   Insofar as the onset of violent passion is not in the individual's power to control, the Captain is in part a victim of natural forces.   (By this I do not wish to diminish his ultimate responsibility, however.   It is clear that he ought to have exercised self-control and not allowed himself to be carried away by his passion.   For the seventeenth-century Catholic dramatists of Spain the free will of the individual was a very real thing.)   We know, however, that although the Captain was full of disdain at first, his curiosity about Isabel was roused because he was told that she had been hidden away from the eyes of the soldiers by her father.   So the chain of causality leads us back to Pedro Crespo. But Isabel must also bear equal responsibility, for when her father tells her to retire, she reveals that she had already decided to do so (I.523-48).

However, Crespo and Isabel are only trying to cope with a situation prudently.   This situation, namely the presence in their house of soldiers, whose reputation for raping peasant-girls was well known, is brought about, in its turn, by a number of subsidiary factors.   The most immediate, and, from the point of view of the mechanics of the plot, the most important, is the Sergeant's act of billeting the Captain on Crespo because the latter's daughter is said to be very beautiful. The Sergeant knows all about the Captain's proclivities and is doing no less than providing the latter with an opportunity for indulging his weakness.

· But there are at least three further factors to be taken into account. The first is this: that soldiers should be billeted at all on Crespo is due to the fact that he refuses to buy a patent of nobility which would allow him to "evade" his duties (I.483-521). The second factor is that the soldiers are billeted in Zalamea because, as we discover in the opening scene, the Town Council accept their obligations and refuse to bribe the soldiers to march on. Here, the Town Council, like Crespo, act rightly, but the consequences in human terms are unpleasant in the extreme. (Compare, also, the intervention of the Council later in the play when they elect Crespo *alcalde*: the consequences of this entirely reasonable decision pose a problem for Crespo, contributing, in the short run, to a temporary loss of his social honour.) The third factor is Lope's order, towards the end of the first act, that the Captain leave Crespo's house and find lodgings elsewhere. It can be argued that this has the effect of making the Captain all the more eager to see Isabel again and even of bringing him to the point of using violence instead of a comparatively harmless stratagem with a pretence of violence.

The implications of all these factors are interesting. In the first place, a series of causal links are established between the deeds of such characters as Crespo, Isabel and Lope and their suffering or frustration. This points in a number of directions: towards pride; towards prudence; and, beyond these, to the nature of the universe.

To take the question of pride first: it is clearly unreasonable to try and establish any serious moral guilt in the intentions and actions of Crespo, Isabel and Lope. Nevertheless, it can be argued that they are all, in some way, guilty of pride. Not that their pride can be regarded as morally evil: indeed, it is largely justifiable. But we are dealing, I think, with the familiar old *hubris* of tragedy, the over-weening pride which almost inevitably leads to a humbling of the characters who possess it.

It is fairly easy to see Crespo as a proud man. He is proud of his social honour: to begin with, he is proud of his status as a peasant, for which there is, of course, a sociological explanation (**15**, pp.107-09). This leads him to refuse to buy a patent of nobility, and, when Juan suggests he do so (I.483ff), he explains that his refusal is a matter of principle with him. To Juan's reasonable counter-arguments, Crespo evinces something of the obstinacy of Juan Labrador of Lope de Vega's *El villano en su rincón*. This perhaps does not quite convince us, though it does silence his son (I.510-21). In any case, we may grant that Crespo's pride is largely justifiable, being based on a sense of moral integrity.

That he is not unconscious of the *molestias* of his status as a peasant, however, becomes clear when he tells Isabel to conceal herself. Now, it is his (albeit justifiable) pride which has led to the soldiers' being billeted on him. To safeguard his social honour, of which he is so proud, he is now compelled to make this further move, which, ironically, contributes in a minor way to Isabel's rape. In other words, the element of pride provides the slight tragic flaw in his character which justifies his suffering. Insofar as Isabel implicitly shares his pride, she, too, is partly responsible for her fate. And both Isabel and her father, by their decision, contribute towards the Captain's ultimate execution.

Juan, too, by wounding the Captain, compels the soldiers to take the latter back to Zalamea, and into Crespo's hands. In this he is aiding the course of justice; but, more interestingly, he is also cutting off one of the Captain's avenues of escape from the consequences of his act. On the other hand, Juan is gaoled by his father for attacking the Captain, though this is ultimately to safeguard his life from the soldiers' vindictive revenge and also from a military tribunal (as well as to give an air of impartiality to Crespo's proceedings). The imprisonment, nevertheless, constitutes a form of dishonour. Juan, as we know, is as proud as his father; he is also impetuous. His pride and impetuosity led him to attack the Captain and for this he is punished. (Ironically, his initial intention was to follow his father's advice by going to the help of a woman —his sister— in distress.) In general, we can say that Juan is lacking in prudence, even though he tries to follow his father's teachings.

Lope, we saw, is also frustrated and his authority defied when Crespo tries, sentences and executes the Captain. But Lope, too, is a proud and impetuous, if just, man. Yet he cannot be acquitted of a certain partiality. He ought to have acted more promptly and energetically against the Captain who, as he knew from the start when Rebolledo revealed all in I.822-29, was after Isabel. In this case, his first words were to condemn Crespo (I.831-33), before confining the soldiers to their quarters for the night. In Act II, after the soldiers are put to flight, Lope is again lenient with the Captain (II.481-85). These are minor points, admittedly, but it is such minor points which contribute to the final tragedy —the Captain's speech about his love, where he stresses that great consequences stem from little beginnings (II. 105ff), applies just as well to the general situation in the play. Furthermore, when we consider that Lope is quite prepared to raze Zalamea to the ground —he makes the threat twice (I.831-33; III.841-44)—, we cannot acquit him of a slight favouritism towards his soldiers and an over-readiness to be harsh towards the civilian population when the two come into conflict. His sense of military honour has not a little to do with his attitude, and this tends in the last analysis to overrule the dictates of prudence.

It would appear, then, that Crespo and his family, as well as Lope, help to bring upon themselves the suffering they undergo towards

the end.   The element of pride in their characters seems to invest
their suffering with a certain poetic justice.   This, of course, does not
lessen the Captain's responsibility, far less his guilt; but we are made
to feel that the other characters who suffer are not wholly innocent
victims.

However, there is another, complementary interpretation which
can be put on the actions of the latter characters.   True, their pride
does create difficult situations for them; but, given this factor, many
of their acts can be seen as prudent attempts to cope with these
situations.   Crespo's concealment of Isabel, for example, can be seen
as an attempt to forestall an unpleasant event: he is clearly not so un-
worldly as to be prepared not to resist evil.   Isabel's agreement with
this, arrived at independently, shows that she is prudent as well as
recatada.   Lope sees that the Captain is billeted elsewhere and also,
in Act II, orders the soldiers to leave Zalamea.   Juan, on the other
hand, is a character who is largely lacking in prudence because of his
youth and consequent lack of experience.   His impetuous acts thus
throw the prudent acts of other characters into relief.

Nevertheless, as events prove, the exercise of prudence is in vain.
The combined efforts of Crespo, Isabel and Lope are unable to avert
the tragedy foreseen.   This is surely the irony A. A. Parker has in mind
when arguing that Isabel is an innocent victim of the Captain's
immoral act and that her fate cannot be seen as poetic justice.[8]   However, as shown above, I myself am inclined to see Isabel's fate as, in
part, a punishment for her own, and, in particular, her father's pride.
Or, to turn the argument round slightly, the element of pride in these
characters has a vitiating effect on their attempts to act prudently.
One can say that their pride either does not allow them to act
prudently enough or blinds them to all the possible consequences of

[8] "Calderón's Rebel Soldier and Poetic Justice", *Bulletin of Hispanic Studies,*
46 (1969), 121.

their actions; moreover, the traditional punishment of *hubris* is intended to underline the fact that man is not master of all things.

Prudence, then, and pride; these are the two interpretations which can be put on so many of the characters' actions. The two are not, as they might at first seem, mutually incompatible: even though they appear to point in different directions, they really stress the multi-faceted nature of the play. Of the two, pride is the less important and ought not to be over-emphasised; by helping us to understand part of the motivation behind the actions, especially those of Crespo and his family, it lessens the sense of outrage we might otherwise feel on witnessing their suffering. The attempt to act prudently, on the other hand, and the largely futile consequences of such actions are much more interesting and disturbing. They lead us on to more difficult terrain.

Crespo's crucial decisions are, if not counter-productive, at least futile. This, we may argue, is coming close to the Aristotelian *hamartia*, an error of judgment. But can we really say that it was wrong? Faced with those circumstances, was there anything else that Crespo and Isabel could have done? And, if not, are we to postulate, in *El alcalde de Zalamea*, a dramatic world ruled by fate akin to that of Greek drama? What makes the problem more acute is the fact that we know that if Crespo had not decided to hide Isabel there is no guarantee that the Captain, given his weakness for a pretty face, would have acted otherwise, and, even if he had done, we can suspect that the Sergeant would have assaulted Isabel (I.199-200). For, later in Act I, we realise that he has been looking for Isabel to flirt with her and has discovered that she has been hidden away (I.577-87). In other words, we realise that the consequences of any decision would have been problematic.

What, then, are the moral lessons contained in the themes of the play? One can say, looking at the tragedy from the point of view of Crespo, that it stresses that moral honour is to be preferred to social honour, which is highly vulnerable. One might also say that it is a warning against pride, especially pride based on social honour. Or one might stress the complementary aspect whereby the play urges us to act prudently and according to the moral law, making us beware of the blinding force of passion and realise the great need to exercise our reason (and, on this level, the play can be seen as a "morality"). All this is true. Yet we are made to realise not only that *hubris* is punished but also that prudence is not necessarily a guarantee against disaster. This is, of course, a rich source of irony in tragedy. But perhaps we can go further. May not the play be using these moral warnings to point to something beyond them, namely the nature of the world in which we live? If we follow this line of thought, we may perceive the philosophical drift of the play, its aim to reveal to us something about the nature of life, which is what all great literature must do.

Let us briefly review what we have discovered about the play. We are presented at the beginning with a number of characters, all proud of their social reputations, all giving us definitions of honour which are in varying degrees inadequate. By the end of the play, all these characters have either lost their honour completely or have felt it to be in some way impugned. As is only reasonable, those whose honour is most substantial (however they define their honour) lose most —Crespo, the Captain—, while those whose concept of honour is hollow —Rebolledo, Mendo— lose least; Mendo, in fact, is cast aside after Act II, since he has nothing to gain and nothing to lose, having had nothing to begin with. The Captain suffers an ignominious death: the fact that he is garotted is a symbolical pointer to his loss of caste, of status, on which he so much prided himself. Crespo, too, loses his social honour which, throughout the play, has been so much prized by him. This, as Dunn has suggested, is the chaff which the wind of God blows away (6, pp.52-53. The reference is to I.433-42). The wheat which remains is, of course, Crespo's own definition of honour as "patrimonio del alma". It is only honour in this sense that

Crespo eventually saves. And he is made to realise what his definition of honour really implies.

There is thus a paradox in the theme, illustrated in the case of Pedro Crespo, whereby moral honour has to be gained from social dishonour. But one must be prepared to accept this. Crespo, by imprisoning Juan and publicly acknowledging Isabel's rape, shows himself prepared thus to renounce his social reputation and to humiliate himself, as he has done earlier on by kneeling before the Captain, which must have been very difficult for such a proud man accustomed to treating people in the same way as they treat him (II.235-44). His reward on earth comes in the form of the title of *alcalde perpetuo*, conferred on him by the King. The King's intervention here is thus patently a *deus ex machina* in the true sense: his action rewards Crespo for his sacrifice, thus going some way to creating God's kingdom on earth. Crespo's frustration and suffering, then, are not unmitigated. Isabel, too, whose fate, more than any other character's, arouses our sympathy, can find consolation only as a bride of Christ. (It is interesting to speculate that the only way of really protecting her from the soldiers would have been to send her, if only for a short period, to a convent.) It is, therefore, only on the religious or quasi-religious level that the prudence of these characters is rewarded. Others, however, such as the Captain, refuse to sacrifice their social honour and suffer much more.

All this points to a further problem. As Dunn has remarked, the play appeals to Law, Nature and Reason (1,p.17). These are necessary for the harmonious working of society. But there is also another dimension to the play: this is its exploration of the nature of freedom, which is linked to the view of the universe presented or implied in *El alcalde*.

W. Kerr has argued an interesting case for seeing tragedy as "an investigation of the possibilities of human freedom".[9] There seems

[9] *Tragedy and Comedy* (London, 1968), p.121.

to me little doubt that Calderón's plays do try to explore the nature of man's freedom, the area of such freedom, and the exercise of it. One feature which would confirm this view is the use of a pattern which occurs over and over again in Calderón's plays: a man is thrown into a situation which requires some response from him. At first, there are several possible ways of meeting the situation; but, as the action progresses, the number of avenues of escape possible is gradually reduced until we find the area in which true freedom can be exercised, the sort of freedom which man in effect possesses, and the way in which he chooses to exercise that freedom.

This pattern is obvious, for example, in another of Calderón's plays, *El príncipe constante*. It will not have escaped anyone's attention that, while there is a considerable amount of physical action in the first half of this play, there is very little in the second half. This is so, as Sloman has pointed out, in order to demonstrate the passive side of fortitude (18, p.192). But what is more pertinent here is the means by which Calderón allows such passive fortitude to be displayed. The action of the play moves systematically from the physical plane to the spiritual, and this is forced on Fernando by a calculated reduction of his physical freedom: from a warrior-prince who has crossed the seas, he becomes a royal captive, courteously treated, then a slave set to work, and finally a prisoner who is no more than a rotting lump of flesh unable to move by himself. This state of utter servitude is brought on him by external forces: the Portuguese lose the battle and Fernando is taken captive; the King is forced to treat him ever more harshly; sickness overtakes Fernando. But it is also partly due to his own decision, first, to fight in the face of overwhelming odds and later, out of a sense of moral integrity, not to accept Muley's offer of help or to flee under any circumstances. Fernando's physical freedom is thus circumscribed, but it is as a slave and on the point of death that he feels himself most free to resist the King openly.

In *La vida es sueño*, too, a similar pattern is traced. Basilio exercises his freedom —wrongly— by imprisoning his son. But in vain. Segismundo, too, at the beginning of the play, bewails his lack of physical freedom. But when he is given this, he only proves to be a slave of his own passions —much as the picaresque heroes do. It is this which is represented symbolically and concretely by his return to the tower. And he is finally free from it only when he has learnt to exercise his free-will rightly.

So, too, in *El alcalde de Zalamea*, the proud Pedro Crespo, perhaps justifiably and rightly proud, is faced with a situation which he sees as a possible threat to his own and his family's honour. He does try to forestall unpleasant consequences, but his action is seen to be futile and can almost be considered as an error of judgment. It is nevertheless a conscious exercise of freedom, a deliberate choice in order to anticipate possible tragedy.

But what is more important is that his measure also fails because the Captain cannot or will not control his passion, and Crespo cannot override the Captain's free-will. That is an area to which his own sphere of freedom to act does not extend.

Lope, too, as we have seen, does not take a strong enough line because of his concern for the honour of the army. Again, Crespo cannot make Lope act otherwise; nor can Lope himself, by his diplomatic hints, dissuade the Captain from his rash deed. Furthermore, as has been argued, Lope's prudent moves in trying to keep the Captain away from Isabel are also counter-productive.

All these factors lead up to the Captain's abduction of Isabel, again a factor of the external world which Crespo has been unable to prevent. But the situation is made more complex by a number of other factors. Crespo's sorrow over his son's departure makes him agree to Inés' suggestion to sit for a while outside the house. Though this suggestion is against Isabel's first impulse, Crespo agrees (II.778-89). Besides, Crespo does not expect the Captain to return. For this

moment's lapse from watchfulness and vigilance, Crespo and his family
have to pay dearly. More, when Isabel is abducted, Crespo finds himself without his sword. Though Inés fetches it for him, he stumbles
and falls as he attacks the aggressors. It is as though fate has conspired
with the Captain in his plan to abduct and rape Isabel.

And yet, as we have seen, Crespo has allowed himself to be caught
—understandably enough, and only for a minute— off his guard.
Eternal vigilance is the price one must pay for an unblemished
reputation; but is this humanly possible? And even if we were to
pass over the question of social honour and simply consider the
question of suffering, we are brutally made aware of man's
vulnerability.

This vulnerability is an integral and inescapable part of Calderón's
view of the world. Man is vulnerable not only because there exist
external events which he cannot control, but also because his own
nature is such that his actions and passions increase his vulnerability
in a world where it is dangerous to act but where action is necessary
and forced on him. So not only does fate conspire with the good
weather to aid the Captain in his dastardly deed, but Crespo's
affection for his son throws him off guard and leaves him open to
attack.

If this were all, we might be outraged rather than made to
experience fear and pity. Why does Crespo send Juan off with Lope?
Juan, it is true, is attracted by the soldiers' life and is presumably eager
to join the army. In granting his son's wishes, Crespo is acting as a
father should and also acting nobly in allowing his son to serve the
King. He does this reluctantly, as his words reveal to us (II.762-68).
But perhaps we remember his earlier proud declaration, insisting that
he and his children are to remain peasants (I.519-21). He may have
come to realise the unreasonableness of his earlier stand, for in his
parting speech of advice to Juan, he seems to hope that Juan will
improve his social status (II.689-96; 741-43). Has Crespo's pride

taken a new turn? If the question is not answered in the play, it is at least raised.

If, up to the end of Act II, Crespo's aim has been to prevent an attack on his honour, now that this has been in vain, his concern in Act III is to seek reparation for this offence. There are a number of choices open to him, but one by one these are all blocked.

The most obvious, simplest and perhaps crudest solution is to do as Isabel expects and kill her. Crespo, of course, is morally right in not killing an innocent girl. But this decision deprives him of one means of clearing his honour. He has exercised his freedom of choice, but by doing so has limited his own freedom of action.

His first thought is to seek out the Captain and kill him in a duel. This, like his decision not to kill Isabel, is a decision freely taken; but this way out, too, is blocked by the news that he has been made *alcalde* (the Town Council here, as at the beginning of the play, being an external "force" pressing on Crespo, although, ironically, Crespo's own virtues are to some extent responsible for his election). As he realises, if he is to perform his duties properly, personal vengeance is now out of the question (III.327-34).

His next move is to beg the Captain on his knees to marry Isabel. This moving episode (III.405-591), seen by Leavitt as a clumsy manoeuvre to ensure that the audience's sympathy goes to the right person,[10] has been, to my mind, correctly interpreted by Dunn (6). The scene is at first sight puzzling, for it seems to reveal an inconsistency in Crespo. He appears to be trying to buy his honour back from the Captain, something which goes clean against his earlier assertion, "que honra no la compra nadie" (I.500). Crespo is indeed prepared to be sold as a slave if that is what the Captain insists on. But, as Dunn argues, Crespo's offer, rather than an attempt at a

---

[10] S. E. Leavitt, "Pedro Crespo and the Captain in Calderón's *El alcalde de Zalamea*", *Hispania* (U.S.A.), 38 (1955), 430-31.

crude business transaction, is no less than an invitation to the Captain to be converted. For the Captain to agree to marry Isabel, he must put away his own social arrogance; this would require his spiritual conversion, which would mean that he ultimately could not accept Crespo's offer to be sold. The conversion appears to the Captain to be too expensive and he refuses. Crespo's last chance of saving his social honour has now been foiled (just as the Captain has thrown away his last chance of saving his life).

Or, perhaps, the sticking-point has now been reached. There is a clear choice open to Crespo and this is the area of his real freedom. He must take a decision which no one else can take for him, and which no outside event, save death, can interfere with. He has to choose between opting on the one hand for his social life and on the other for his moral life. That is, considering his social honour too important to lose, he can try to save it by attempting to hush up the matter: Isabel can be sent to a convent and Crespo can determine to brave out any gossip or slander. But this would not only imply living a lie —which would be hardly possible for the Pedro Crespo who knows that a wig cannot hide a man's baldness (I.503-12)—, but would also mean a dereliction of duty by letting the Captain escape scot-free. No; to be true to himself as a man and as an *alcalde*, Crespo must punish the Captain for his crime. But, in order to do this, he must renounce, as we have seen, all his social honour.

The dilemma of having to choose between the social and the moral life, between the good of the body and the good of the soul, is a recurrent one in Calderón's plays. In his wife-murder plays, the husband consistently chooses his social life; but Calderón does not fail to point to the folly, futility and absurdity of this misguided exercise of an individual's freedom. Such is the case in, for example, *El médico de su honra* and *El pintor de su deshonra*. In these plays, murder achieves little or nothing; true, the husband can continue to live in society; but one wonders whether he finds his life worth living. Juan Roca, in *El pintor de su deshonra*, makes it clear that he no longer wishes to live, though society insists that he do so as an "honourable" man.

On the other hand, the man whose honour has been attacked can decide to renounce his social honour in order to do the morally right thing. This is what happens in *El alcalde de Zalamea*. Crespo chooses to save his moral life, which means losing his social life. Not only does Crespo's choice involve the loss of his social honour; it can-not avoid or remove suffering either. Isabel's life in society is rendered impossible. Crespo's, too, might have been, were it not for the King's timely *deus ex machina* intervention. Dunn has rightly stressed the powerlessness of Justice to avoid or cure suffering (1, p.23). We may add that not even obeying God's law or acting prudently is any guarantee against suffering. It is the Christian view of this world that life is a Cross each man must bear.

One is therefore led to conclude that in Calderón's dramatic world neither the choice of social values nor that of moral ones can lead men to happiness. Happiness and safety, for Calderón, are not to be found on this earth —at least not while human nature is what we know it to be. And if suffering and death are the only inescapable and, indeed, the ultimate facts of life, what must guide man must be thought for his soul.

So, while Dunn is right in arguing that the play deals with the importance of Law, Nature and Reason, I feel that it stresses the more pessimistic view of things: if only men observed the Law, if only they exercised their Reason responsibly, if only they acted in harmony with Nature, life on earth would be happier. Agreed; but can they? The play seems to me to point to the ambivalence of Nature, the inadequacy of Law, and, perhaps especially, the inadequacy of Reason.

Calderón's world is unpredictable, and, perhaps, from a religious point of view, this is as it should be. Its unpredictability at once warns us of our own vulnerability and clarifies for us the area of the individual's freedom. This is tiny, but crucial; it, too, is part of the unfixed, unbound element in the universe. To use this freedom responsibly is the problem of the individual; yet it is not reason but faith which is of importance in deciding how to act at the crucial moment. Crespo calculates, even errs; the Captain, too, calculates, and also errs. But Crespo draws the right lesson from his experience, while the Captain does not. To obey the teaching of religion, to do what is morally right, these are the only things which can save us in this world. But if we are saved, it is not *for* this world.

VI

Form and Structure

As I observed in the Introduction, Calderón, like all his contemporaries, used the form fixed by Lope de Vega for the *comedia*: this was in three acts and in verse of different metres. The basic conventions of this form, which were fairly firmly established by the time Calderón started to write in the early 1620's, were non-classical in nature: the three unities were not observed; tragic and comic elements were mixed; the tragic hero was not necessarily of noble birth, etc.

As Sloman has pointed out, however, Calderón, while accepting the non-classical form of the *comedia*, tends to produce plays of a more classicising cut than his predecessors (**18**, p.297). This was in part due to the criticisms of the literary theorists, but also in part —and perhaps more importantly— to Calderón's desire to write more coherent, unified plays. Most of the devices employed to ensure greater unity were essentially structural devices, and will be discussed presently.

But it is interesting to note first how, as regards formal features, *El alcalde de Zalamea*, as in so many other ways, is within as well as outside Calderón's own normal dramatic conventions. It is, of course, in three acts, in verse, and employs a variety of metres. As is normal in the *comedia*, the change of metre coincides with a change of scene or mood or tempo. Most of the metres are based on the octosyllabic line, save for the scene of the first clash between Crespo and the Captain (I.557-680), where the Italianate hendecasyllable and heptasyllable take over. Again, as is normal, tragic and comic elements are mixed, although one gets the impression that the tragic mood predominates, while the comic effect belongs mainly to the first two acts and centres around the antics of Mendo and Nuño on the one hand and, on the other, the scenes with Rebolledo and Chispa. Indeed, in the final act, Mendo and Nuño disappear, and the humour of the short scene with Rebolledo and Chispa is obviously forced, as is appropriate in the circumstances. The protagonist, Crespo, is not of noble birth, but, as has been pointed out (22, p.155), this is exceptional in Calderón, though characteristic of many of Lope de Vega's plays. As Sloman stresses, however, Crespo, though not a nobleman, is morally noble, Calderón having thus dignified the peasant of the source play. As regards the three unities, the play, to some extent, observes the unity of place, the action occurring in Zalamea and its environs. The unity of time, however, is violated, and I shall return to this later. The unity of action is basically maintained, even though the vestigial secondary action concerned with Mendo and Nuño could be dispensed with from the point of view of action. But, in accordance with A. A. Parker's principle, from the thematic point of view these two characters are of considerable importance.

To turn to the structure, it is here that what is most typical of Calderón, namely the artificiality of his art, becomes evident. This may be a surprising statement, for the play has so often been praised for being "realistic". The realism is, of course, there, but as with so much else in the theatre, it is largely a cleverly produced illusion.

A. A. Parker has drawn attention to the extreme artificiality of the dramatic structure of *El alcalde de Zalamea* (12). As he has shown, each act of the play can be divided into six dramatic divisions. In Act I, the first unit introduces the atmosphere of military life —carefree and undisciplined. This is the thematic introduction of disorder. The exposition is completed by the addition of new elements, the structure thus being a logical, cumulative one. The first of the new elements is the Captain, introduced in the second unit. He, too, belongs to the disorderly life of the soldiers. Mendo and Nuño, introduced in the third unit, complete the picture of aristocratic pride, giving us a caricature of the concept of true nobility. The fourth unit introduces to us Crespo, Juan and, later, Isabel. Crespo and Juan contrast, as Parker says, with the two types of *hidalgo* so far presented. Crespo is rich because, unlike Mendo, he works. Again, unlike Mendo and the Captain, Crespo and Juan see nobility consisting in what one really is. With the presentation of the most important characters, the stage is set for the conflict between the peasants and soldiers, which begins in the fifth unit. In the final unit, Lope arrives to put an end to the quarrel. He arrives last, Parker argues, because the maintenance of law and order is the basic theme. Lope is the representative of authority and, as such, criticises Crespo. Lope, then, is to defend the external forms of justice, while Crespo is to defend its inner essence. The latter will have to fight against not only the Captain, but also the law, the authority of the army and, therefore, of the state.

Act II is also divided into six units, which, in turn, are symmetrically subdivided into two ternary groups. In each of the two latter groups, we get, first, a scene of disorder or the characters who represent it; next, the forces of social order; and thirdly, the clash of the two elements. In the first half of the act, we learn that Mendo is keeping watch while Álvaro decides to serenade Isabel. The second unit consists of the supper scene. The serenade begins. The third unit is the *riña.*

This basic pattern is repeated in the second half of the act. As Mendo and Nuño go off, Álvaro and the soldiers return, to be ordered to leave by Lope. In the fifth unit, we get Crespo's advice to Juan and the amicable farewell between Lope and Crespo. In the sixth unit, the Captain returns and abducts Isabel, the act ending with its second *riña.*

Act III is also in six sections, but there is a return to the pattern of Act I, in which the principal characters appear in succession. The main difference is that Crespo remains on stage almost from the beginning, and has to face the problems set for him by each character. In the first dramatic unit, the climax of the play is reached. The rape of Isabel is revealed, and therefore Crespo's dishonour. The latter's problem is how he, as a peasant, is to obtain justice. In the second unit, Crespo is brought face to face with the problem. While Isabel expects to be killed, Crespo says and does nothing because, as Parker says, he is thinking about the safety of his son. (Here, I prefer to lay the stress on Crespo's initial resolve to kill the Captain.) But he is elected *alcalde* and is now responsible for the execution of justice. The third unit is the confrontation between Crespo and the Captain, which ends in the latter's arrest and imprisonment. In the fourth unit, Crespo imprisons Juan who wants to kill Isabel. This at once punishes Juan, safeguards his life and prevents the killing of Isabel. The fifth unit brings Lope back to Zalamea, producing a confrontation of two men who refuse to yield. Crespo has undermined Lope's authority and the latter orders his men to attack the town. In the final unit, the King appears. Crespo is now brought into conflict with the King, who, however, appoints Crespo *alcalde* for life.

The structure of the play, then, as Parker insists, is far from realistic. There is a structural rigidity in terms of the number six, which helps to present the theme clearly and powerfully. Parker does not think that this division was an accident, although it may not have been consciously worked out in detail by Calderón. Structural symmetry, argues Parker, may have become a habit of mind with Calderón. But what is remarkable is that this rigidity does not spoil the play; its natural and "realistic" appearance, in spite of its artificiality, is a triumph of Calderón's art.

Such is A. A. Parker's argument. But his main point of an extreme artificiality underlying an apparent realistic spontaneity is one which is equally applicable to other aspects of the play. Sloman has pointed out, as mentioned above, that Calderón moves towards a greater observance of neo-classical precept, even if this is achieved by deliberately leaving such things as time and place vague. As regards the unity of place, this, as has been said, is largely observed. But, as Sloman has argued, Calderón, at the opening of the play, uses a shifting-setting technique, the setting following the action continuously.[11] This technique is repeated later, as for example at the beginning of Act III.

The question of time is perhaps even more intriguing. As I have tried to show elsewhere (8), the action begins in the light of mid-afternoon and moves into darkness. The final act moves from darkness (it opens just before dawn) into light. The psychological effect, therefore, is that the unity of time is maintained, that is, the action of the play appears to take place during a period of twenty-four hours. That much of the action in Act II takes place during night-time adds to this effect.

In actual fact, close scrutiny reveals that the action of the play is spread over four days (or three twenty-four-hour cycles). Act I begins in mid-afternoon of the first day and ends at night. Act II covers two days: it begins just before night-fall on day 2, which ends with the clash between Crespo and Lope and the soldiers. The rest of Act II takes place during the third day. Act III begins just before sunrise on day 4 and ends later that same day.

The handling of the passage of time is therefore far from "realistic": it involves an extremely artificial time-sequence, which is highlighted by the frequent references in the text to the time of day. This curious handling of time is intended to ensure that the main crises in the play occur at night. These are: the first quarrel between Crespo and the soldiers with which the first act ends; the second quarrel in the middle of Act II; and the abduction and rape of Isabel, which

[11] A. E. Sloman, "Scene Division in Calderón's *Alcalde de Zalamea*", *Hispanic Review*, 19 (1951), 66-71.

take place at the end of Act II. Calderón, in other words, deliberately distorts the passage of time in the play in order to exploit the light-darkness symbolism which is such a characteristic feature of much of his drama. I shall discuss this symbolism in slightly greater detail in the following chapter when I analyse the imagery in the play.

VII

Style

Stylistically, as in so many other respects, *El alcalde de Zalamea* appears to stand apart from Calderón's other plays in being more "realistic". A good example of such stylistic realism is provided by the complaints of the soldiers with which the play opens. The same easy, natural style is continued even when Crespo and his son come on stage.

But, on closer inspection, it becomes obvious that this apparently natural style is highly contrived. The artificiality of the style of *El alcalde de Zalamea* is not immediately obvious, hence the view of Menéndez y Pelayo that Isabel's long speech at the beginning of Act III is a stylistic flaw (**10**, p.227). In actual fact the stylistic texture of this speech is not very different from that of many other passages in the play.

Take, for example, the question of imagery. True, Isabel's speeches are full of images, especially of images of nature. But they are not unique. In *El alcalde*, imagery tends to occur in periodic bursts, the effect of this being to make us more conscious of the images when they do appear. Compare, for instance, the sudden outburst of images in the Captain's speeches in II.75-116, which vividly convey the strength of the sudden passion that will bring about his destruction. Yet it is not merely at moments of high emotional intensity that the language of the characters becomes more image-laden. The imagery in *El alcalde*, as in all of Calderón's plays, is strictly functional and is intended to reinforce the basic themes of the work. Hence the images of violence and of fire in its destructive aspects in the Captain's speech.

Similarly, Crespo's description of his farm in I.424-42 is not intended as a mere splash of local colour. It is the first extended speech with obvious images in the play, and this invites us to concentrate on its implications. There are a number of points to be noted concerning this speech. The most obvious is Crespo's pride in his grain, the product of his husbandry. But he describes it in terms of gold standing out against the blue of the sky. These are, of course, natural colours, for Crespo's wealth consists of the gifts of Nature won from her by hard work, and they are meant to contrast with the blue and gold paint of Mendo's *ejecutoria* (I.262-63), a useless bit of parchment inherited by the latter from his ancestors without any work on his part or any effort to deserve it. But just as Mendo is proud of his *ejecutoria*, in which his social honour consists, Crespo is proud of his wheat-fields, on which his social honour is founded. In other words, honour for Mendo is based on inherited social status; for Crespo it is based on the natural dignity of man achieved by dint of hard work and personal effort. At the end of this speech, Crespo refers to the possible threat of a storm. E. M. Wilson has drawn attention to Calderón's use of the four elements in his imagery (20). The orderly separation of the elements indicates a state of cosmic harmony. Disharmony, on the other hand, is suggested, as in this speech of Crespo's, by a confusion of the elements. On an obvious level, the confusion anticipated is the Captain's rape of Isabel which brings about Crespo's loss of honour. But the storm is also a natural phenomenon, just like the wheat, and should be seen, to some extent, as an act of God. Crespo, as I suggested in an earlier chapter, is a proud man, proud of his social honour, which is here symbolised by the wheat. He intends to safeguard it against any possible attack, which is an act of prudence. But man's contingency planning is not always adequate, for there are unpredictable forces in the world, some of them stronger than man, as Crespo himself realises (I.439-42). His seclusion of Isabel, as subsequent events prove, is in vain, for Providence has a lesson to teach him.

Later on, in II.183-210, there is a lyrical description of Crespo's garden. Again, this is much more than a piece of "realistic" description. The peace which pervades the scene is meant to clash violently with the earlier speeches of the Captain with their images of violence. The subdued, natural music of the fountain —concordant music, in literature of this period, almost always symbolises harmony[12]— throws into contrast the raucous serenade which we learn is being prepared (II.135-82) and which is heard soon afterwards (II.319ff). The fact that this scene is set in a garden is also significant. It draws attention to the order and harmony consonant with Crespo's view of life and thus is opposed to the *monte* which, as Dunn points out (1, p.8), is Álvaro's retreat and the scene of violence.[13]

What has been said so far about the imagery is enough to prove that it has a thematic and structural function in the play. Descriptions and settings, therefore, are not primarily "realistic", but essentially symbolic. This fundamentally artificial nature of the imagery is confirmed by the light-darkness symbolism employed by Calderón.

As is frequently the case in his plays, light signifies honour and harmony, darkness, dishonour and discord (13). Thus, Calderón so manipulates the passage of time in *El alcalde* that the three crucial steps in the dishonouring of Crespo take place at night. Similarly, honour is associated with light. A good example is the final scene of the play in which the King confers on Crespo the honour of *alcalde perpetuo* and which takes place in daylight. Also, honour is consistently described in images of light: compare, for example, Crespo's speech to Juan (II.687-88).

---

[12] For the symbolic use of music, see J. W. Sage, "Calderón y la música teatral", *Bulletin Hispanique*, 58 (1956), 275-300, and for a more general survey, L. Spitzer, *Classical and Christian Ideas of World Harmony* (Baltimore, 1963).

[13] For a discussion of the symbolic function of imagery in Golden Age drama, see J. E. Varey, "La campagne dans le théâtre espagnol au XVIIe siècle", in *Dramaturgie et Société: Rapports entre l'oeuvre théâtrale, son interprétation et son public aux XVIe et XVIIe siècles*, Vol. I, ed. J. Jacquot (Paris, 1968), pp.47-76.

Nevertheless, it will be observed that the equations light = harmony and darkness = discord do not appear to be constant. A good example of a discrepancy is the dinner-scene in the middle of Act II. This is enclosed between the Captain's decision to serenade Isabel and the actual serenade which leads to a brawl in the street. These two events are evidently scenes of social and moral discord and thus take place, appropriately, at night. But the dinner-scene is clearly indicative of a mood of harmony, of peace, and of a certain reconciliation between Crespo and Lope; and it, too, takes place at night. The symbolism is therefore ambiguous, but this is not, I think, a case of oversight on Calderón's part. The basic theme, as I have argued, rests on the paradoxical birth of honour out of dishonour: Crespo's discovery of the full meaning of moral honour comes about as a result of his social dishonour. Thus, while the play can be seen in one sense as the story of the dishonouring of Crespo (leaving aside for the moment, the final, redeeming honour conferred on him at the end in which the King appears, as I have argued, as a *deus ex machina*), it is simultaneously, in another sense, a dishonouring which serves to reveal the true nature of honour. This ambiguity in the play seems to me to be faithfully reflected in the ambiguous use of light-darkness symbolism.

Imagery is not, of course, the only stylistic aspect worth examining. As is well known, the Spanish *comedia* employs a variety of metres, each being considered suitable for a particular mood or situation. I shall not here discuss the different metres used in *El alcalde*, since this aspect can readily be explored by the interested student, apart from mentioning that it is worth while training one's ear (and eye) to recognise changes in metre, since these normally herald a change in scene, or more importantly a change in situation, tone or mood. Note, for example, the switch from the "natural" *romance* to the more "artificial" *silva* in I.557-680, a scene of action, deception and incipient violence. The *silva* is, of course, an Italianate verse-form and its use here (the only use, incidentally, of an Italianate metre in the play) can be seen as introducing the first real clash between a more artificial —and false— set of values and a more "natural", true set. This symbolic use of verse-forms can be compared with the symbolic exploitation of a conventional style in I.349-52: here, Mendo's use of trite *culto* imagery and an equally trite play of wit reveals his vacuous mentality.

There are, however, other stylistic and metrical aspects of the play worth considering. Two of these, in particular, draw attention further to the highly artificial style of Calderón. The first is the standard device of *diseminación-recolección*, discussed by Dámaso Alonso.[14] A good example is to be found in the Captain's speech in II.105-16. Here, in the last three lines (114-16) are gathered ("recollected") the basic images introduced singly ("disseminated") in the first part of the speech (105-12). The same device is employed in the Captain's earlier speech in II.75-92. In these two speeches, not only does the profusion of images increase the poetic "tension", but it will be noted that the later speech stresses images of violence, while the earlier one (75-92) stresses the changing nature of things (of which the Captain is at the moment prepared to consider only the favourable aspect —although the irony of the play is that just as unhappiness is followed by happiness, so is happiness followed by sorrow).

The second point we should note is the extremely stylised form of the altercation between Crespo and Lope in I.850-94. Dámaso Alonso has pointed out that the two men are, in fact, saying the same things in slightly different ways, Crespo echoing and capping Lope's utterances. Dunn has stressed, on the other hand, that the stylization of the dialogue draws attention to the fact that the two men are saying quite different things, using roughly the same words (**6**). In actual

[14] "La correlación en la estructura del teatro calderoniano", Chapter 4 in D. Alonso and C. Bousoño, *Seis calas en la expresión literaria española*, 3rd ed. (Madrid, 1963), pp. 109-75. This book is an important work for the study of Spanish literary style.

fact, both Alonso and Dunn are probably correct. Both Crespo and Lope are emphasising their individual claims to possess honour. They differ, however, in their definitions of honour: for Lope, honour is essentially an external social phenomenon, based on social class and privilege; for Crespo, honour is, of course, something moral, that is, "patrimonio del alma".

The stylistic device noted here recurs later on: for example in II. 183ff and again in III.779ff. The purpose in each case is rather different. But these points draw attention to the overall "artificiality" of the style of this play, and make us realise that its natural, "realistic" nature is not a spontaneous phenomenon or an attempt to capture the reality of everyday language, but a deliberately calculated device which has a specific function within the play. In style and language, as in all other respects, *El alcalde de Zalamea* is an exquisite artifact.

VIII

Staging

There is nothing unusual about the staging of *El alcalde*, but it does exemplify Calderón's mastery of his physical medium in his exploitation of the resources of the contemporary stage. Stagecraft is essentially an art of creating illusion. But the nature of the theatre probably made the creating and maintaining of illusion rather more difficult in Calderón's day than in our own, even making allowances for the fact that the seventeenth-century audience was undoubtedly conditioned to accept the theatrical conventions of the time.

Let us briefly consider the Golden Age stage and the conditions under which plays were performed. (For an exhaustive discussion of this, see **17.**) The stage in the *corrales* or public theatres was not the picture-frame stage with which we are familiar today, but, like the English Elizabethan stage, an apron stage which jutted out into the audience. At the back there was a central recess, which could be curtained off. This could be used for discoveries, etc. There were doors on either side to provide the normal entrances and exits. At the first-floor level, there were windows which opened onto a balcony. This could represent the balcony of a house, or town-walls, or a mountain. Access to it was by means of staircases. The whole stage, then, presented much the same appearance as the inner façade of a house (which, of course, it historically was). There were no sets and consequently no scenery. Much care and expense went on costumes, however, even though they were largely conventionalised and were, in fact, more elaborate forms of seventeenth-century dress.

Performances were held in the afternoon, in broad daylight. There was no artificial lighting to eke out the attempt to create an illusion.

Night was indicated by the use of appropriate dress and also by bringing tapers on stage.

Incidentally, these conditions may very well have helped to counteract to some extent the theatrical illusion and remind the audience that what it was witnessing was a play and not events from real life. Thus Golden Age drama, as C. A. Jones has pointed out, probably had some points in common with Brecht's dramatic theory of alienation, which requires the audience to be kept constantly aware of the fact that it is seeing a play.[15] This breaks the theatrical illusion and facilitates a critical response on the part of the audience to the action on stage.

The seventeenth-century audience was, however, critical enough. It was a heterogeneous assembly and not composed mainly of members of certain social classes —if only because the theatre was one of the principal forms of public entertainment of the day. This meant that the plays had to appeal to different levels of intelligence, in other words, that they had to have different levels of meaning. Each sector of the audience would expect to be catered for, and it was very vocal in its protests if it thought it was being slighted. The most critical sector, as is to be expected, was the noisy *mosqueteros* or groundlings, who came armed with missiles, vocal as well as material. It required a very skilful dramatist to satisfy their demands, without, at the same time, disappointing the more sophisticated spectators.

The seventeenth-century stage had many positive advantages, but, as I have suggested, it also had many disadvantages. Its intractable aspects no doubt offered a challenge to the dramatist's skill. Let us see how Calderón met this challenge in *El alcalde de Zalamea.*

The first problem was to attract the audience's attention and impose silence (which, of course, could not be done by dimming the

[15] "Brecht y el drama del Siglo de Oro en España", *Segismundo*, Nos. 5-6 (1967), 39-54.

lights). The opening of the play with the loud tramp-tramp of the soldiers succeeds perfectly in doing this. Next, the colourful sight of the army compels the eye's attention. Finally, the first words are the complaints of the ill-tempered Rebolledo, no doubt shouted at the top of his voice.

The next, and perhaps more important, problem would be to retain the audience's interest in the play for two more hours. The story and themes help to do this; but the more theatrical aspects are no less important. Costume is important: as we recall, it is one of the few details not left entirely to the spectator's imagination. Juan is impressed by the Captain's uniform (I.565-66). Crespo and his family would be dressed as wealthy but not socially pretentious peasants. Mendo's appearance would be as grotesque as his mentality, and, as Calderón points out, he and his servant are meant to conjure up Don Quijote and Sancho Panza.

Perhaps an even more important factor is stage action. There is much of this in the play. There is, for example, the feigned quarrel between Rebolledo and the Captain towards the end of Act I; the fight between Crespo and the soldiers in the middle of Act II; the abduction of Isabel at the end of Act II; and so on. The tempo of the action is skilfully varied, alternating between bouts of action and set pieces such as Crespo's advice to Juan and Isabel's soliloquy at the beginning of Act III. Music and songs (some of them popular ditties) would also help to retain the audience's interest.

Most of the action of the play takes place on the stage proper. Shifts of scene are fairly frequent; but since there were no sets to change, the scene often shifts continuously. As Sloman points out, the scene changes at the opening of Act I from the road to Zalamea to just outside Zalamea without the soldiers leaving the stage at all. [16]

[16] A. E. Sloman, "Scene Division in Calderón's *Alcalde de Zalamea*", *Hispanic Review*, 19 (1951), 66-71.

They would simply march round and round the stage. This technique ensures flexibility and continuity in the flow of action. What we might see as a defect, that is, the absence of sets, is thus converted into a positive dramatic virtue.

Moreover, another result of the absence of sets is the fact that language is used to establish the scene at any particular moment when this is felt to be necessary. Thus there is a certain amount of word-painting —compare Juan's description of the wood in which he is lost at the end of Act II, which is, of course, also symbolic—, and a consequent enhancement of the poetic qualities of the language. Furthermore, the audience is thereby called on to exercise its imagination to the full, which ensures a hold on its attention and its active involvement in the drama being enacted before its eyes.

Not only is the physical setting indicated in the language, but also the time of day or night, if this is important. There are, as has been pointed out, very many references to time in the play, and the action alternates between night and day.

If the above points serve to indicate how Calderón turns the short-comings (as we see them) of his stage to advantage, we must also consider how he exploits its more positive features. A good instance is his use of the physical structure of the stage to reinforce parallels. Parallelism of character is reinforced, for example, in I.403-16 when Crespo and his son, Juan, come on stage from different directions but react in the same way to Mendo's presence, using similar language. (At the same time, entering from different directions, they provide an elementary bit of humour by making it impossible for Mendo to slink away: he is compelled to brave it out.) But that Crespo and Juan enter through different doors subtly points to a difference between father and son which will become clearer as the action progresses. Another interesting example is in II.426-58, when Lope and Crespo come on stage, again through different doors, each putting to flight some of the soldiers, then turning back to see that all is clear, catching sight of each other, approaching, challenging and fighting each other in the front centre of the stage. The language again reinforces this similarity but also hints at a difference. As we have seen, Crespo's and Lope's views of life, though in large part similar, are, at bottom, ultimately irreconcilable: a meeting between them must be a confrontation, not a dialectical conflict which has any possibility of achieving a synthesis of reconciliation.

The inner recess of the stage is brought into use a number of times in the play. It is here that the important dinner-scene (II.183ff) takes place; here, too, Crespo has his interview with the Captain (III.390ff). It is also used for two dramatic discoveries: Isabel's discovery of her father, bound to a tree (III.79) and the final discovery of the garrotted Captain (III.910), a most effective *coup de théâtre* which forms the catastrophe.

The balcony represents the window of Crespo's house in I.353 from which Inés and Isabel catch sight of the ridiculous Mendo below in the street, and at which the soldiers aim their songs and pebbles in II.332ff; and it represents the attic of the house in I.681ff.

These examples help to illustrate Calderón's unobtrusive mastery of his physical medium. He can turn to positive advantage what seem to us shortcomings of the stage of his time. Just as important is his skill in bringing out all its resources. But we feel that these are used naturally and inevitably, with restraint and tact, not to provide us with a show of technical virtuosity.

IX

Conclusion

The above chapters, I hope, will have given some idea of the present state of views on Calderón's *El alcalde de Zalamea* and also, perhaps, help to explain why this play has continued to exercise such a hold on successive centuries.

Admittedly, the recent increased interest in it is not due to the same reasons as those which prevailed in the nineteenth century. Menéndez y Pelayo was impressed, above all, by its "realism", which, in his eyes, made it exceptional in the vast body of Calderonian artificial drama. The present day, less concerned with a narrowly-defined realism, has turned again to Calderón, finding his "artificiality" rightly worthy of attention. This new appreciation of Calderón, which involves accepting him on his own terms, has helped us to see *El alcalde de Zalamea* in a new light. As I hope I have pointed out, this play not only possesses a highly attractive surface realism, but is also as artificial as any of Calderón's other works; nor is it lacking in symbolic elements. It is also a convincing demonstration of Calderón's mastery of his theatrical medium and helps to confirm his excellence as a playwright.

The issues with which the play is concerned are of no less interest. In the political context of the seventeenth century, Crespo's reiteration of the need to keep Caesar and God distinct is subtly subversive. The exaltation of the morally noble peasant also has its political and social implications in the seventeenth century. In the atmosphere of the present-day world in which the conflict between the individual and a complacent, at times unjust, authority is pointed, Crespo's assertion of the inherent dignity of the individual and the permanent superiority of the moral law to the law of the state and to social conventions is by no means a dead and dated topic. And the illustration of the possibly disastrous consequences to the individual of subordinating expediency and self-interest to principle and morality reveals much about the ultimate nature of tragedy.

Selected Critical Bibliography

Editions

1. Calderón de la Barca, Pedro. *El alcalde de Zalamea.* Ed. P. N. Dunn. Oxford: Pergamon Press, 1966. Based on the earliest (Alfay) printed edition (Alcalá, 1651), this is the only modern critical edition of the play intended for English readers.
2. Calderón de la Barca, Pedro. *El alcalde de Zalamea.* Ed. J. Geddes. Boston: Heath and Co., 1918. This is based on Krenkel's eclectic edition of 1887. The Introduction is slight and inadequate, and, while the editor preserves the unjustifiable nineteenth-century practice of dividing the acts into scenes, the text is very readable.
3. Calderón de la Barca, Pedro. *La vida es sueño* and *El Alcalde de Zalamea.* Introduction and Notes by S. E. Leavitt. The Laurel Language Library. New York: Dell, 1964. Introduction slight. Some interesting points —e.g., says Crespo's concealment of Isabel ironically arouses the Captain's curiosity (p.15)—, but not developed. Text based on Vera Tassis edition of 1683.

Criticism

4. Casanova, W. O. "Honor, patrimonio del alma y opinión social, patrimonio de casta en *El alcalde de Zalamea*, de Calderón." *Hispanófila*, año undécimo, tercer número, No. 33 (May, 1968), pp.17-33.
An interesting article which rightly stresses the importance of social honour in the play. It is slightly marred by a too close adherence to Américo Castro's rather narrow view of honour.
5. Cotarelo y Mori, E. *Ensayo sobre la vida y obras de Don Pedro Calderón de la Barca.* Reissued. Madrid, 1924.

Perhaps still the standard life-and-works, but outdated in some respects.

6. Dunn, P. N. "Honour and the Christian Background in Calderón." *Bulletin of Hispanic Studies*, 37 (1960), 90-105. Reprinted in Wardropper (**19** below), pp.24-60. References are to this latter reprint.

An important article which presents honour as a form of false religion. Perhaps goes just a little bit too far. (The necessary corrective view is to be found in Peristiany, **15** below.) The second section of the article is an excellent study of *El alcalde* in the light of the theoretical premises set out in the first part. Stresses the view that *El alcalde* provides a critique of the code of honour, and a humane, moral solution to a problem of honour. Again, this view is slightly overdeveloped. Casanova (**4** above) restores the balance.

7. Dunn, P. N. "Patrimonio del alma." *Bulletin of Hispanic Studies*, 41 (1964), 78-85.

An interesting gloss on Crespo's famous definition of honour, bringing out its legalistic overtones. See also **6** above.

8. Halkhoree, P. "The Four Days of *El alcalde de Zalamea*." To be published in *Romanistisches Jahrbuch* in 1972.

An attempt to show how the paradox in the theme of the play is reflected in the ambivalence of the light-darkness symbolism and how the latter demands a highly artificial management of the time-sequence.

9. Hesse, E. W. *Calderón de la Barca.* Twayne's World Authors Series 30. New York, 1967.

The latest general introduction to Calderón's works. Competent but often light-weight. The analysis of *El alcalde* is not very probing.

10. Menéndez y Pelayo, M. *Calderón y su teatro.* Buenos Aires, 1946. First published Madrid, 1881. All references are to the 1946

reprint.

This book, originally a series of lectures on Calderón delivered in 1881, probably did most to stunt the growth of a genuine appreciation of Calderón in Spain. Ostensibly seeks to praise Calderón; instead, often damns with equivocal praise. Hostile to the "artificial" aspects of Calderón's drama. A good example of the nineteenth-century naive, "realistic" approach to literary criticism. Singles out *El alcalde* for praise as, artistically, the best of Calderón's works.

11. Parker, A. A. *The Approach to the Spanish Drama of the Golden Age.* Diamante Series VI. London, 1957. All references are to the 1964 reprint.

A formulation of principles to aid in the study and appreciation of Golden Age drama. Most of the best work on the *comedia* and especially on Calderón (especially by British Hispanists) is indebted, positively or negatively, to this small booklet. Though plenty of exceptions can be found to the principles, their application to a play is certain to cast some light on it. For a survey and critique of this and some of Parker's later works, see Pring-Mill (**16** below).

12. Parker, A. A. "The Dramatic Structure of *El alcalde de Zalamea*." Lecture delivered at the Instituto de España, London, in 1969. To be published shortly.

A brilliant analysis of the structure of the play. See Chapter VI for a summary of the argument of this paper.

13. Parker, A. A. "Metáfora y símbolo en la interpretación de Calderón." *Actas del primer congreso internacional de hispanistas* Oxford, 1964, pp. 141-60.

An important study of imagery, etc. in Calderón's drama.

14. Parker, A. A. "Towards a Definition of Calderonian Tragedy." *Bulletin of Hispanic Studies*, 39 (1962), 222-37.

An examination of a particularly Calderonian type of tragedy in which "diffused responsibility" (the unwitting, not necessarily evil acts of many characters) lies at the root of the catastrophe. Points out that the suffering of innocent victims of another's wrongdoing is not to be seen as poetic justice.

15. Peristiany, J. G., ed. *Honour and Shame: The Values of Mediterranean Society*. London, 1965.

A collection of essays by various authors on the phenomenon of honour. Very important as an analysis made by sociologists. Of crucial importance for the student of Spanish Golden Age literature are the first two essays: "Honour and Social Status," by J. Pitt-Rivers (pp.19-77), and "Honour and Shame: A Historical Account of Several Conflicts," by J. Caro Baroja (pp.79-137).

16. Pring-Mill, R. D. F. Review of A. A. Parker: *The Approach to the Spanish Drama of the Golden Age* (London, 1957). *Romanistisches Jahrbuch*, 13 (1962), 384-87.

A critical review of A. A. Parker's work on the theory of the *comedia* (especially **11, 14** above).

17. Shergold, N. D. *A History of the Spanish Stage from Medieval Times until the End of the Seventeenth Century*. Oxford, 1967. Now the standard work on the subject, superseding all previous works.

18. Sloman, A. E. *The Dramatic Craftsmanship of Calderón: His Use of Earlier Plays*. Oxford, 1958.

A crucial work which disposed once and for all of the traditional charge that Calderón plagiarised other dramatists. Sloman compares Calderón's plays with their sources, bringing out the nature of his "dramatic craftsmanship" by showing how his *refundiciones* are much superior artistically and more profound thematically. Chapter 8 (pp.217-49) deals specifically with *El alcalde*.

19. Wardropper, B. W., ed. *Critical Essays on the Theatre of Calderón*. New York, 1965.

A collection of some of the most important articles on Calderón written in this century by British and American critics.

20. Wilson, E. M. "The Four Elements in the Imagery of Calderón." *Modern Language Review*, 31 (1936), 34-47.

    Crucial for the understanding of the thematic function of Calderón's imagery.

21. Wilson, E. M. and Moir, D. *A Literary History of Spain: The Golden Age: Drama 1492-1700*. London and New York, 1971.

    A good general survey. A brief reference to *El alcalde* on pp.111-12.

22. Wilson, M. *Spanish Drama of the Golden Age*. (Oxford, 1969).

    A general survey of Golden Age drama. A very good account on the whole. Some controversial views along with a number of perceptive comments.